Second Book of Oboe Solos

Zweites Spielbuch für
Oboe und Klavier

Edited and arranged for Oboe and Piano by
JANET CRAXTON and ALAN RICHARDSON

Faber Music Limited
London

Preface

This collection follows directly on the *First Book of Oboe Solos*, both technically and musically.

As in the First Book certain principles have been adhered to in the choice of pieces and in the way that we have edited and arranged them. Many of the pieces are cantabile in nature: good singing tone with equally good intonation are in our opinion two of the most important assets of an oboist. This is often harder to attain in certain keys than others and to give extra practice we have used all the keys up to 4 sharps and 4 flats.

Again, we have in general tried to help the oboist by providing resting places — not only for breathing, but to allow time to relax and reform the embouchure, so very important for good tone production.

While we have made editorial suggestions for phrasing, dynamics, etc. in the 17th century and 18th century pieces that we have arranged, we should be happy if students and teachers felt free to use their own initiative here. In all the original compositions, however, and the Grieg and Schumann arrangements the phrasing and dynamics should be very meticulously observed. We are grateful to the late Harold Craxton for his arrangement of *O Mistris Myne*.

Let us repeat the importance of beautiful phrasing, not just in the short slurs, etc., but in the overall shaping of the longer phrases. Remember the connection between music and speech. The musical phrase, like the sentence in speech, has to be shaped to make the meaning clear. Never play any music without intent. Always try to understand the mood of the music, i.e. whether it is gay, sad, reflective, energetic, etc., so that you can make this apparent to the listener.

We have arranged these pieces in approximate order of difficulty and generally adding a new note every two or three pieces. These notes may well have occurred previously in scales and exercises, but now there will be the opportunity of playing them in different conditions.

If the oboist is also a pianist, it would be advantageous for him or her to play the piano parts with a fellow oboist.

Short footnotes to each piece are included, which we hope may prove helpful.

JANET CRAXTON
ALAN RICHARDSON

© 1972 by Faber Music Ltd
First published in 1972 by Faber Music Ltd
3 Queen Square London WC1N 3AU
Cover design by M & S Tucker
Printed in England by Halstan & Co Ltd

Separate oboe parts are available

Vorwort

Diese Sammlung schließt sich spieltechnisch und musikalisch direkt an das *Erste Spielbuch für Oboe* an.

Wie im Ersten Spielbuch, so hielten wir uns auch hier an bestimmte Grundsätze bezüglich der Wahl der Stücke und der Art und Weise, wie wir sie herausgegeben und bearbeitet haben. Viele der Stücke sind kantabler Natur: ein guter singender Ton und eine gleichermaßen gute Intonation sind, unserer Meinung nach, zwei der wichtigsten Qualitäten eines Oboisten. Diese sind in gewissen Tonarten oftmals schwieriger zu erlangen als in anderen, und, um zusätzliches Übungsmaterial zur Verfügung zu stellen, haben wir alle Tonarten bis zu 4 Kreuzen und 4 Bs verwendet.

Wiederum haben wir im allgemeinen versucht, den Oboisten durch die Bereitstellung von Pausenstellen zu unterstützen – nicht nur zum Atmen, sondern auch um ihm Zeit zu gönnen, den Ansatz zu entspannen und neu zu formen, was so äußerst wichtig für eine gute Tonerzeugung ist.

Obwohl wir in den von uns bearbeiteten Stücken aus dem 17. und 18. Jahrhundert editorische Vorschläge hinsichtlich Phrasierung, Lautstärkeangaben usw. gemacht haben, würden wir uns freuen, wenn Schüler und Lehrer sich nicht scheuten, hier eigene Initiative zu zeigen. In allen Originalkompositionen jedoch und in den Bearbeitungen der Stücke Griegs und Schumanns sollten die Phrasierungs – und Lautstärkeangaben sehr gewissenhaft befolgt werden. Wir sind dem verstorbenen Harold Craxton für seine Bearbeitung von *O Mistris Myne* zu Dank verpflichtet.

Laßt uns nochmals auf die Bedeutung hinweisen, die eine schöne Phrasierung nicht nur für die kurzen Bögen usw., sondern auch für die Formung ganzer längerer Phrasen hat. Halte dir den Zusammenhang von Musik und Rede vor Augen. Die musikalische Phrase muß, genau wie der Satz in der Rede, gestaltet werden, damit ihre Bedeutung klar wird.

Spiele niemals Musik, ohne dabei etwas zu beabsichtigen. Versuche stets, die Stimmung der Musik zu verstehen, d.h. ob sie lustig, traurig, nachdenklich, energisch usw. ist, damit du dies dem Zuhörer deutlich machen kannst.

Wir haben diese Stücke nach ungefähr fortschreitendem Schwierigkeitsgrad angeordnet und im allgemeinen alle zwei oder drei Stücke eine neue Note hinzugefügt. Diese Noten können sehr wohl früher in Tonleitern und Etüden vorgekommen sein, jetzt jedoch besteht die Gelegenheit, sie in anderen Zusammenhängen zu spielen.

Ist der Oboist zugleich Pianist, so wäre es für sie oder ihn von Vorteil, die Klavierstimme für einen anderen Oboisten zu spielen.

Jedem Stück wurden kurze Anmerkungen beigefügt, die sich, so hoffen wir, als nützlich erweisen mögen.

JANET CRAXTON
ALAN RICHARDSON

Contents : Inhalt

1. AYRE

Melodie

JOHN BLOW
(1649-1708)

*Play thus:

2. A DANCE-FRAGMENT
Ein Tanz-Fragment

ALAN RICHARDSON

3. FIRST LOSS
Erster Verlust

ROBERT SCHUMANN
(1810-1856)

4. RONDEAU
(from *A Midsummer Night's Dream*)

HENRY PURCELL
(1659-1695)

* **Play thus:** (The tie between the B's may be omitted.)

5. O MISTRIS MYNE
O meine Herrin

WILLIAM BYRD
(1543-1623)
arr. H.C.

6. POETIC TONE-PICTURE, No. 5
Poetisches Tongemälde Nr. 5

EDVARD GRIEG
(1843–1907)

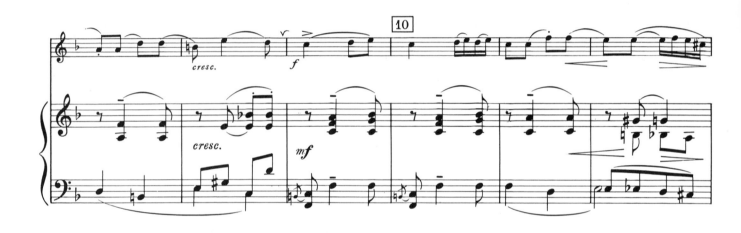

7. AIR
Melodie

ALAN RICHARDSON

8. THEME: LA CI DAREM LA MANO

WOLFGANG AMADEUS MOZART
(1756-1791)
arr. Beethoven

9. A FOURPENNY FABLE
Ein Fünfpfennigmärchen

ALAN RICHARDSON

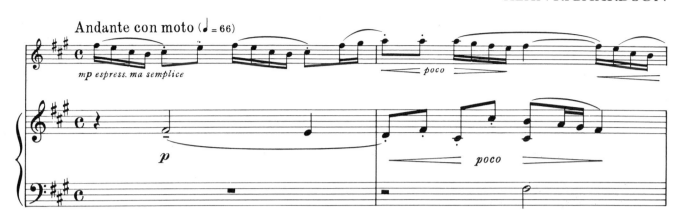

10. ARIETTA

EDVARD GRIEG
(1843-1907)

II. SEA SHARP
Narciss

ALAN RICHARDSON

12. ARIA
Arie

GEORGE FRIDERIC HANDEL
(1685-1759)

13. SONG FROM THE HILLSIDE

Lied vom Bergabhang

ALAN RICHARDSON

14. AFFETTUOSO

(from *Sonata in C minor*)

GEORG PHILIPP TELEMANN
(1681-1767)

15. ALLEGRO

(from *Sonata in C minor*)

GEORG PHILIPP TELEMANN
(1681-1767)

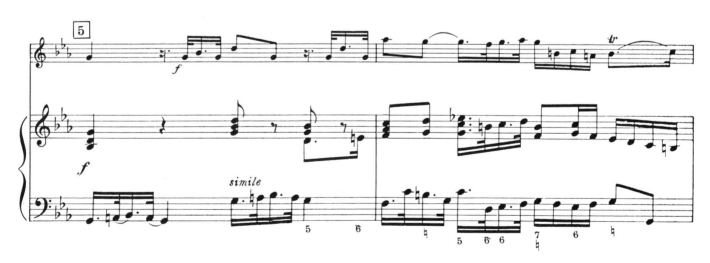

17

16. A MELODY FOR DAVID

Eine Melodie für David

ALAN RICHARDSON

Andante: piacevole e semplice

17. MISS BAKER'S HORNPIPE

(from *The Compleat Tutor for the Hautboy*)

ANONYMOUS
(c. 1770)

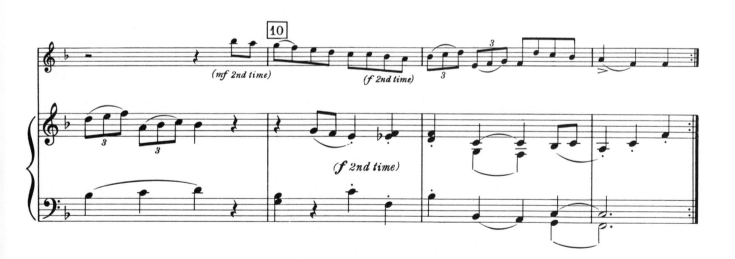

18. LOVELY NYMPH

Liebliche Nymphe

(from *The Compleat Tutor for the Hautboy*)

ANONYMOUS
(c. 1770)

*Play thus:

Second Book of Oboe Solos

Zweites Spielbuch für
Oboe und Klavier

Edited and arranged for Oboe and Piano by
JANET CRAXTON and ALAN RICHARDSON

OBOE PART

Faber Music Limited
London

Preface

This collection follows directly on the *First Book of Oboe Solos*, both technically and musically.

As in the First Book certain principles have been adhered to in the choice of pieces and in the way that we have edited and arranged them. Many of the pieces are cantabile in nature: good singing tone with equally good intonation are in our opinion two of the most important assets of an oboist. This is often harder to attain in certain keys than others and to give extra practice we have used all the keys up to 4 sharps and 4 flats.

Again, we have in general tried to help the oboist by providing resting places — not only for breathing, but to allow time to relax and reform the embouchure, so very important for good tone production.

While we have made editorial suggestions for phrasing, dynamics, etc. in the 17th century and 18th century pieces that we have arranged, we should be happy if students and teachers felt free to use their own initiative here. In all the original compositions, however, and the Grieg and Schumann arrangements the phrasing and dynamics should be very meticulously observed. We are grateful to the late Harold Craxton for his arrangement of *O Mistris Myne*.

Let us repeat the importance of beautiful phrasing, not just in the short slurs, etc., but in the overall shaping of the longer phrases. Remember the connection between music and speech. The musical phrase, like the sentence in speech, has to be shaped to make the meaning clear. Never play any music without intent. Always try to understand the mood of the music, i.e. whether it is gay, sad, reflective, energetic, etc., so that you can make this apparent to the listener.

We have arranged these pieces in approximate order of difficulty and generally adding a new note every two or three pieces. These notes may well have occurred previously in scales and exercises, but now there will be the opportunity of playing them in different conditions.

If the oboist is also a pianist, it would be advantageous for him or her to play the piano parts with a fellow oboist.

Short footnotes to each piece are included, which we hope may prove helpful.

JANET CRAXTON
ALAN RICHARDSON

Contents : Inhalt

1. AYRE
Melodie

JOHN BLOW
(1649–1708)

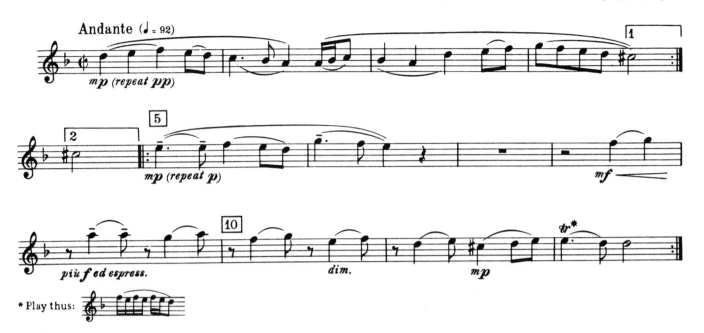

* **Play thus:**

New note: A above the stave.

The long phrase-marks here show the overall lengths of the phrases; make the joins between the shorter slurs as legato as possible but give clear definition to the notes marked ⌢. Both repeats should be played. To help the rhythm in bars 9-11, think at first in quavers but take care that there are no bulges on the crotchets. When using the 2nd octave key make as little movement of the hand as possible—the slightest rocking action is all that is required. The trill in the last bar can be played faster than suggested provided the quaver D is full length (the piano trill in bar 8 should conform to the oboe trill).

Neue Note: A über dem Notensystem.

Die langen Phrasierungsbögen zeigen hier die Gesamtlänge der Phrasen an. Mache die Verbindungsstellen zwischen den kürzeren Bögen so legato wie möglich, spiele jedoch die durch ⌢ gekennzeichneten Noten klar und bestimmt. Beide Wiederholungen sollten gespielt werden. Denke, um mit dem Rhythmus in den Takten 9-11 besser zurechtzukommen, zunächst in Achteln, passe jedoch auf, daß die Viertel dann kein Anschwellen im Ton zeigen. Bewege die Hand bei der Verwendung der zweiten Oktavklappe so wenig wie möglich – eine äußerst geringe Schaukelbewegung, das ist alles, was verlangt ist. Der Triller im letzten Takt kann schneller als vorgeschlagen gespielt werden, vorausgesetzt, daß dem Achtel D der volle Wert gegeben wird (der Klaviertriller in Takt 8 sollte dem Oboentriller entsprechen).

2. A DANCE-FRAGMENT
Ein Tanz-Fragment

ALAN RICHARDSON

New note: low C.
Let this flow along. The phrasing is important: ⌒ means give a melodic stress to the first note and shorten the second without tongueing it. You can use a very soft tongueing action between the slurs especially at bars 3-4 and 9-12. Begin the piece with sufficient tone in *mf* to allow room for a good contrast when you come to the *p* in bar 9. Always remember that dynamics are relative, and therefore in most cases it is the contrast that is important. Use a very round embouchure (lip formation) for the low C.

Neue Note: tiefes C.
Lasse dieses Stück dahinfließen. Die Phrasierung ist wichtig: ⌒ bedeutet: gib der ersten Note einen melodischen Akzent und verkürze die zweite, ohne sie anzustoßen. Zwischen den Bögen, besonders in den Takten 3-4 und 9-12, kannst du einen sehr sanften Zungenanstoß verwenden. Beginne das Stück mit genügender Tonstärke in *mf*, um Spielraum für einen guten Kontrast zu lassen, wenn du zum *p* in Takt 9 kommst. Vergiß nicht, daß Lautstärken relativ sind, und daß daher in den meisten Fällen der Kontrast das wichtige ist. Verwende für das tiefe C einen sehr runden Lippenansatz.

3. FIRST LOSS
Erster Verlust

ROBERT SCHUMANN
(1810-1856)

Try to make the *fps* expressive rather than hard. They should sound rather like deep quick sighs, and should not be so very much stronger than the up-beat to bar 25. The last 4 bars plus up-beat quaver should, of course, start strong and almost angry.

Versuche, die *fps* eher ausdrucksvoll als hart zu spielen. Sie sollten mehr wie tiefe, schnelle Seufzer klingen und nicht sehr viel stärker sein als der Auftakt zu Takt 25. Die letzten 4 Takte zusammen mit dem Achtel des Auftakts sollten natürlich energisch und beinahe zornig beginnen.

6

4. RONDEAU

(from *A Midsummer Night's Dream*)

HENRY PURCELL
(1659-1695)

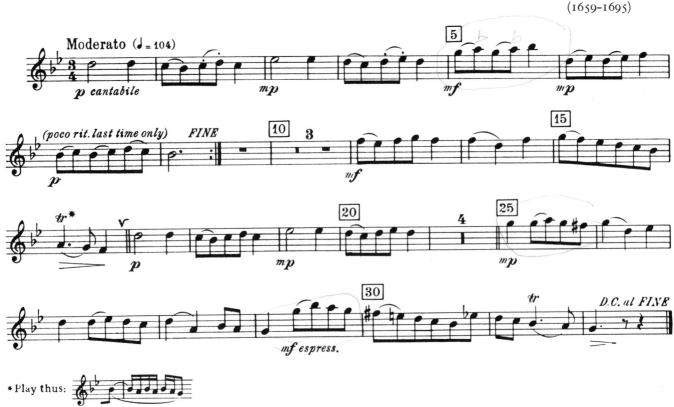

* Play thus:

New note: B flat above the stave.
Oboist and pianist should take great care to phrase alike here. Try playing the Da Capo very quietly throughout with a diminuendo over the last 4 bars, remembering that quiet playing requires plenty of firm support from the diaphragm. The trills may be played as shown or faster, provided the quaver after the trill is full length.

Neue Note: B über dem Notensystem.
Oboist und Pianist sollten sich große Mühe geben, hier überein-stimmend zu phrasieren. Versuche, das Da Capo durchweg sehr leise zu spielen, mit einem diminuendo in den letzten 4 Takten, wobei du daran denken mußt, daß leises Spiel viel starke Unterstützung vom Zwerchfell erfordert. Die Triller können wie angegeben oder schneller gespielt werden, vorausgesetzt, daß das Achtel nach dem Triller seinen vollen Wert behält.

5. O MISTRIS MYNE

O meine Herrin

WILLIAM BYRD
(1543-1623)
arr. H.C.

Very legato tongueing is needed throughout this lovely piece. Remember that it is a song and needs to be played as you would sing it. The notes may seem simple but to give full beauty and meaning to them requires much thought, very careful listening and considerable breath and lip control. If you find a diminuendo on the low G difficult, try adding your E flat key (and even the F key as well), which will help to keep the pitch up and give you confidence to diminuendo.

Während dieses ganzen Stückes braucht man einen sehr legato Anstoß. Denke daran, daß es ein Lied ist und so gespielt werden muß, wie du es singen würdest. Die Noten mögen einfach erscheinen; es bedarf jedoch guten Überlegens, viel aufmerksamen Zuhörens und beachtlicher Atem – und Lippenkontrolle, um ihnen volle Schönheit und Bedeutung zu geben. Wenn du ein diminuendo auf dem tiefen G schwierig findest, mache den Versuch, deine Es-Klappe (und sogar auch die F-Klappe) mitzuverwenden, die dabei helfen wird, die Tonhöhe oben zu erhalten und dir Selbstvertrauen zum diminuendo geben wird.

6. POETIC TONE-PICTURE, No. 5
Poetisches Tongemälde Nr. 5

EDVARD GRIEG
(1843–1907)

Play the grace-note acciaccaturas (bars 6 and 13) rather quickly but very clearly, and finger them out (no trill keys!). The breath marked in bar 8 should be taken very quickly and must not disturb the crescendo. (Listen to the way good singers snatch a breath without breaking a phrase.) Practise the semiquaver passage in bar 14 until you get it very smooth and clean. This piece could be repeated without a rit the first time.

Spiele die ornamentalen Acciaccaturen (Takte 6 und 13) ziemlich schnell, aber sehr klar, und greife sie (keine Trillerklappen verwenden!). Das Atemholen, das in Takt 8. angegeben ist, sollte sehr schnell geschehen und darf das crescendo nicht stören. (Höre dir an, wie gute Singer schnell Atem holen, ohne die Phrase zu unterbrechen.) Übe die Sechzehntelpassage in Takt 14, bis du sie sehr flüssig und sauber spielen kannst. Dieses Stück könnte wiederholt werden, wobei man das rit. beim erstenmal wegläßt.

7. AIR
Melodie

ALAN RICHARDSON

All the pieces so far have been in the most usual time-signatures, with 2, 3, 4 or 6 beats to a bar. However, composers quite often write in 5/8 or 7/8, etc.; none of us has any difficulty in counting up to 5 or 7, so playing this correctly should not present too much of a problem. Just be careful that you *do* think in 5.

Alle bisherigen Stücke hatten die gebräuchlichsten Taktangaben, mit 2,3,4 oder 6 Zählzeiten pro Takt. Komponisten schreiben jedoch ziemlich oft in 5/8 oder 7/8 usw.; keiner von uns hat irgendwelche Schwierigkeiten bis 5 oder 7 zu zählen, und so sollte es kein zu großes Problem sein, dieses Stück richtig zu spielen. Passe lediglich auf, daß du *tatsächlich* in 5 denkst.

8. THEME: LA CI DAREM LA MANO

WOLFGANG AMADEUS MOZART
(1756-1791)
arr. Beethoven

This is the theme from *Don Giovanni* that Beethoven used for his *Variations* for two oboes and cor anglais. We hope that one day you will have the chance of playing the whole work in its original form, and also the Trio in C, Op.87. We suggest the grace-note acciaccatura in bar 4 should be played just before the beat. You will probably have to snatch a breath in bar 18, but be careful not to interrupt the flow of the phrase. Start by playing the trills in bars 22 and 24 as suggested. When your fingers become more agile you can add more notes to the trill, using the trill key in bar 24.

Das ist das Thema aus *Don Giovanni*, das Beethoven für seine *Variationen* für zwei Oboen und Englischhorn verwendete. Wir hoffen, daß du eines Tages die Gelegenheit haben wirst, das ganze Werk in seiner Originalfassung zu spielen, und ebenso das Trio in C, op. 87. Wir schlagen vor, daß die ornamentale Acciaccatura in Takt 4 knapp vor der Zählzeit gespielt wird. Du wirst wahrscheinlich in Takt 18 schnell Atem holen müssen; passe jedoch auf, daß du den Fluß der Phrase nicht unterbrichst. Spiele die Triller in den Takten 22 und 24 anfangs wie vorgeschlagen. Wenn deine Finger flinker werden, kannst du mehr Noten in den Triller aufnehmen und in Takt 24 die Trillerklappe verwenden.

9. A FOURPENNY FABLE
Ein Fünfpfennigmärchen

ALAN RICHARDSON

New note: B above the stave.
Play this cantabile but be very careful of the phrasing. The staccato quavers should not be too short. If you can hear an untidy sound between B and C sharp in the middle of the instrument, make up some exercises for yourself using these notes legato. This, of course, applies to any other combinations of notes over the break, such as C-D, C-E flat, B-D, etc. To obtain a good round quality of tone on the B above the stave, you must avoid pinching with the embouchure and give plenty of support from the diaphragm.

Neue Note: H über dem Notensystem.
Spiele dieses Stück cantabile, aber achte sehr auf die Phrasierung. Die Stakkatoachtel sollten nicht zu kurz sein. Schreibe dir, wenn du einen unsauberen Klang zwischen H und Cis in der Mitte des Instruments hörst, selbst ein paar Übungen auf, die diese Noten legato verwenden. Dies gilt natürlich auch für alle anderen Notenkombinationen über dem Registerwechsel, wie C-D, C-Es, H-D usw. Um beim H über dem Notensystem eine gute, runde Tonqualität zu erreichen, mußt du viel Unterstützung vom Zwerchfell geben und es vermeiden, mit dem Lippenansatz zu quetschen.

10. ARIETTA

EDVARD GRIEG
(1843-1907)

Play the mezzo-staccato notes ⌢⌢⌢ as cantabile as you can without losing the definition. Remember that if you are playing in a resonant hall or room more definition (or separation) is needed than in a small, heavily curtained and carpeted room. Listen for the grace-notes in the piano part leading into the 13th and the last bars.

Spiele die Mezzostakkato-Noten ⌢⌢⌢ so cantabile wie du es vermagst, ohne daß die Noten an Präzision verlieren. Denke daran, daß, wenn du in einem widerhallenden Saal oder Raum spielst, mehr Präzision (oder Trennen der Noten) vonnöten ist, als in einem kleinen Raum mit schweren Vorhängen und dicken Teppichen. Horche auf die Verzierungsnoten in der Klavierstimme, die in den 13. Takt und die letzten Takte leiten.

11. SEA SHARP
Narciss

ALAN RICHARDSON

New note: low C sharp.

You will probably notice that low C sharp has a quality different from its neighbours, especially from C and D. It is not usually one of the oboe's best-sounding notes and needs a lot of 'nursing' to improve its quality. For all low notes it is necessary to use a very round embouchure, but for C sharp it must be a *very* round one!

Neue Note: tiefes Cis.

Du wirst wahrscheinlich bemerken. daß das tiefe Cis eine von seinen Nachbarnoten, vor allem C und D, verschiedene Tonqualität hat. Es ist in der Regel nicht eine der bestklingenden Noten auf der Oboe und braucht eine Menge "Pflege" zur Verbesserung seiner Qualität. Bei allen tiefen Noten ist es notwendig, einen sehr runden Ansatz zu verwenden, für das Cis jedoch muß es ein *sehr* runder sein!

12. ARIA
Arie

GEORGE FRIDERIC HANDEL
(1685-1759)

Ornamentation of melodic lines (such as trills, turns, any added decorations or variations) was customary in Handel's day, and if the player did not ornament it would be assumed that the composer had failed to inspire him! We have suggested some possible ornaments and variants in the repeats and recommend that eventually you try to make versions of your own. Remember that whatever you play must fit with the keyboard-part (i.e. the harmony) and that it should be in the style of the piece. It will help if you play the piece several times in its original form before you add much, apart from trills or mordents. When you have become familiar with this procedure, try to make ornamented repeats for the *Ayre* by John Blow (No. 1), and also for the Da Capo of Purcell's *Rondeau* (No. 4) and later for the *Affettuoso* by Telemann (No. 14).

Verzierungen von melodischen Linien (wie Triller, Doppelschläge, jegliche hinzugefügte Ausschmückungen oder Variationen) waren zu Händels Zeiten üblich, und wenn der Spieler keine Verzierungen spielte, wurde angenommen, daß es dem Komponisten nicht gelungen war, ihn zu inspirieren! Wir haben einige mögliche Verzierungen und Varianten in den Wiederholungen vorgeschlagen und empfehlen, daß du schließlich versuchst, eigene Versionen anzufertigen. Denke daran, daß alles, was du spielst, zur Klavierstimme (d.h. der Harmonie) passen muß, und daß es im Stil des Stückes sein sollte. Es wird von Nutzen sein, wenn du das Stück einige Male in seiner originalen Fassung spielst, bevor du, abgesehen von Trillern, Pralltrillern und Mordents, viel hinzufügst. Wenn du mit dieser Verfahrensweise vertraut bist, könntest du versuchen, verzierte Wiederholungen für das *Ayre* von John Blow (Nr. 1), und ebenfalls für das Da Capo von Purcells *Rondeau* (Nr. 4) und später für das *Affettuoso* von Telemann (Nr. 14) anzufertigen.

13. SONG FROM THE HILLSIDE
Lied vom Bergabhang

ALAN RICHARDSON

New Note: C above the stave.
Let this piece flow along without being fast. Notice how the music begins on the 2nd beat of the bar thus giving it a slightly unusual rhythmic feeling.

Neue Note: C über dem Notensystem.
Lasse dieses Stück dahinfließen, ohne zu hasten. Beachte, wie die Musik auf der zweiten Zählzeit des Taktes beginnt und ihm so ein leicht ungewöhnliches rhythmisches Gefühl verleiht.

14. AFFETTUOSO
(from *Sonata in C minor*)

GEORG PHILIPP TELEMANN
(1681-1767)

Affettuoso means affectionately and, although it is not a tempo indication that we use now, it was used often in Telemann's day, particularly by Telemann himself. It is not a fast tempo and an andante quaver beat would be right here.

A special word to the pianist (and oboist). We have given the figured bass, indicating the harmony, here and in the Allegro following. The custom in Telemann's day would have been for the keyboard player to play from the figured bass only and for him to harmonize (realize) the part as he went along. We have given a suggested realization. Always remember that the bass line is a duet with the solo part and should be dynamically equal to it, but the right hand part must be at least one dynamic degree down from this, except where the solo part is resting.

Affettuoso bedeutet innig, und obwohl es keine Tempoangabe ist, die wir jetzt gebrauchen würden, wurde es zu Telemanns Zeiten oft als solche verwendet, besonders von Telemann selbst. Es ist kein schnelles Tempo, und ein Andante, gezählt in Achteln, wäre hier richtig.

Ein besonderes Wort an den Pianisten (und Oboisten). Hier und in dem folgenden Allegro haben wir den bezifferten Baß, der die Harmonie bezeichnet, angegeben. Zu Telemanns Zeit wäre es für den Spieler des Tasteninstruments Brauch gewesen, nur vom bezifferten Baß zu spielen und beim Spielen selbst die Stimme zu harmonisieren (auszusetzen). Wir haben eine von uns vorgeschlagene Aussetzung des Basses angegeben. Vergiß nie, daß die Baßlinie ein Duett mit der Solostimme darstellt und ihr von der Lautstärke her entsprechen sollte; die Stimme der rechten Hand muß jedoch wenigstens einen Lautstärkegrad leiser sein, außer wenn die Solostimme eine Pause hat.

15. ALLEGRO
(from *Sonata in C minor*)

GEORG PHILIPP TELEMANN
(1681-1767)

Make the rhythm here very vital and pointed, with the dotted notes almost double dotted. Notice the many changes of mood and make these changes very clear by playing the dolce sections very dolce to contrast with the precise rhythmic figuration.

Gestalte den Rhythmus hier sehr lebendig und pointiert, und spiele die punktierten Noten fast doppelt punktiert. Beachte die vielen Stimmungswechsel und bringe diese Wechsel sehr deutlich heraus, indem du die dolce Abschnitte im Gegensatz zu der präzisen, rhythmischen Figuration sehr dolce spielst.

16. A MELODY FOR DAVID
Eine Melodie für David

ALAN RICHARDSON

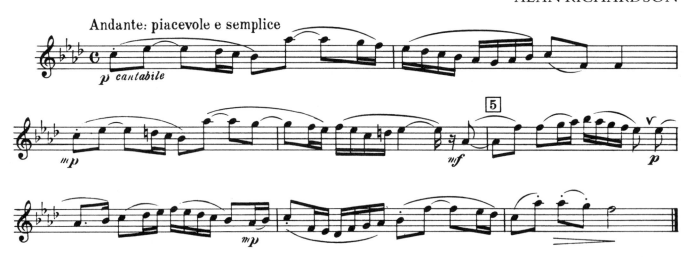

In bars 1, 3 and 7 we find another mezzo-staccato figure ; the C should be slightly lifted and separated from the following note which needs gentle tongueing. Remember to use your L.H. E flat key whenever the E flat precedes or is preceded by D flat. Match the sounds and intonation of the notes throughout so that we hear no unwritten accents or stresses.

In den Takten 1, 3 und 7 finden wir eine weitere Mezzostakkato-Figur ; das C sollte leicht angehoben und von der folgenden Note getrennt werden, die einen sanften Zungenanstoß verlangt. Vergiß nicht, die Es-Klappe der linken Hand immer dann zu verwenden, wenn das Es einem Des vorangeht oder nachfolgt. Stimme die Klänge und Intonationen der Noten durchweg aufeinander ab, so daß wir keine nicht angegebenen Akzente oder Betonungen hören.

17. MISS BAKER'S HORNPIPE
(from *The Compleat Tutor for the Hautboy*)

ANONYMOUS
(c. 1770)

If you find any of the passage-work difficult, try practising it in different rhythms, while retaining the written phrasing.

Bars 5-8, for example: ♩ ♪ ♩ ♪ etc. and ♩ ♪ etc.

So long as you keep the rhythms very tight and your fingers very relaxed, this should quickly help you to improve your finger technique. All detached quavers and crotchets should be played rather short.

Solltest du einige der Passagen schwierig finden, so mache den Versuch, sie in verschiedenen Rhythmen zu üben, wobei du die angegebene Phrasierung beibehältst. Takte 5-8 z.B. usw. Und usw.

Solange du die Rhythmen sehr genau einhältst und die Finger sehr entspannst, sollte dir dies schnell dabei helfen, deine Fingertechnik zu verbessern. Alle nicht gebundenen Achtel und Viertel sollten ziemlich kurz gespielt werden.

18. LOVELY NYMPH

Liebliche Nymphe

(from *The Compleat Tutor for the Hautboy*)

ANONYMOUS
(c. 1770)

*Play thus:

This theme requires the utmost singing-tone and legato phrasing; again it gives good practice in using the L.H. D sharp key. Don't forget that you will need plenty of firm support from the diaphragm in your *pp* phrase at the end. If you fail to provide enough support the phrase will sound tentative and frail instead of controlled and quiet.

Für dieses Thema benötigt man einen äußerst singenden Ton und eine gebundene Phrasierung; es stellt wiederum eine gute Übung in der Verwendung der Dis-Klappe der linken Hand dar. Vergiß nicht, daß du in deiner pp Phrase am Ende viel kräftige Unterstützung vom Zwerchfell brauchen wirst. Wenn du nicht genug Unterstützung zur Verfügung stellst, wird die Phrase wie ein Versuch und schwach, anstatt kontrolliert und leise klingen.

19. FRIENDSHIP
Freundschaft
(from *Studies in General Bass*)

GEORG PHILIPP TELEMANN
(1681-1767)

The changes of time, from 2/4 to 3/8 and from 3/4 to 9/8, may present some difficulties at first. To ensure that the quavers are equal in value (♪ = ♪), begin by thinking in quavers throughout until the changes become familiar. Pianists should take special care to count 9 quavers in bar 14.

Die Taktwechsel von 2/4 nach 3/8 und von 3/4 nach 9/8 werden anfangs vielleicht einige Schwierigkeiten bereiten. Um dafür zu sorgen, daß die Achtel gleichwertig sind (♪ = ♪), solltest du zunächst durchweg in Achteln denken, bis die Wechsel vertraut sind. Die Pianisten sollten in Takt 14 besonders darauf achten, daß sie 9 Achtel zählen.

20. AIR
Melodie

HENRY PURCELL
(1659-1695)

One of our favourite melodies in this book, this *Air* must be played with great control, and above all with the umost love and affection. The trills in bar 20 and 23 could be played as in the *Rondeau* (No. 5) or you can trill faster and stop on the dot (in this case the 2nd beat). When you play the repeat don't forget to try some ornaments and variants.

Dieses *Air*, eine unserer Lieblingsmelodien in diesem Buch, muß mit großer Kontrolle, und vor allem mit größter Liebe und Zuneigung gespielt werden. Die Triller in den Takten 20 und 23 können so wie im *Rondeau* (Nr. 5) gespielt werden, oder du kannst schneller trillern und auf dem Verlängerungspunkt aufhören (in diesem Fall der 2. Zählzeit). Vergiß nicht, einige Ornamente und Varianten zu probieren, wenn du die Wiederholung spielst.

21. HORNPIPE
(from *A Midsummer Night's Dream*)

HENRY PURCELL
(1659-1695)

This *Hornpipe* will make a good pair with the *Air* (No. 20) for concerts, private or public. The trills can be fast and should stop on the dot. In each case make a slight diminuendo from the trill through the following two notes.

Dieser *Hornpipe* und das *Air* (Nr. 20) werden zusammen ein gutes Paar für Konzerte zu Hause und in der Öffentlichkeit abgeben. Die Triller können schnell sein und sollten auf dem Verlängerungspunkt aufhören. Spiele jedesmal ein leichtes diminuendo vom Triller über die nächsten zwei Noten hinweg.

22. ADVENTURE IN STACCATO
Abenteuer in Stakkato

ALAN RICHARDSON

This is just what the title suggests. The tempo can be increased as you get better at controlling your staccato-playing.

Dies ist genau das, worauf der Titel anspielt. Du kannst das Tempo mit fortschreitender Kontrolle deines Stakkatospiels beschleunigen.

23. DOWN THE VALLEY
Das Tal hinunter

ALAN RICHARDSON

New note: C sharp above the stave (see Appendix).
Here you have an opportunity to begin a piece without any accompaniment. Try taking a little rhythmic licence (rubato).

Neue Note: Cis über dem Notensystem (siehe Anhang).
Hier hast du eine Gelegenheit, ein Stück ohne Begleitung zu beginnen. Mache den Versuch, dir eine kleine rhythmische Lizenz zu erlauben (rubato).

24. L'AMOUR DE MOI

FRENCH TRADITIONAL
arr. A.R.

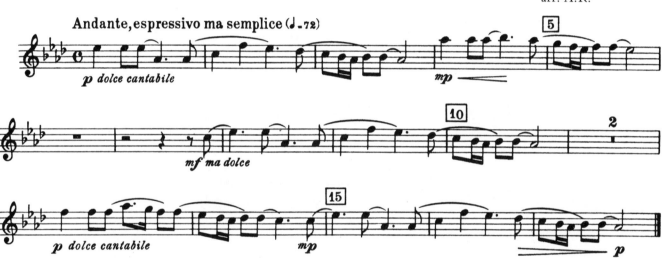

A beautiful melody, but not such a comfortable key! Take great care of the intonation and tone-quality throughout. If your low A flat sags when played quietly, try adding your E flat key. This can help, but beware of it making the note too bright in quality.

Eine schöne Melodie, aber keine so bequeme Tonart! Gib dir mit der Intonation und der Tonqualität durchweg viel Mühe. Mache, wenn dein tiefes As beim Leisespielen im Ton absinkt, den Versuch, deine Es-Klappe hinzuzunehmen. Das kann Abhilfe schaffen, aber paß auf, daß es die Note nicht zu hell klingen läßt.

25. GERECHTER GOTT, ACH, RECHNEST DU?

(from *Cantata No. 89*)

JOHANN SEBASTIAN BACH
(1685–1750)

*Play thus: **

This aria from Cantata No. 89 is for soprano, oboe obbligato and bass continuo. Obbligato means in this context 'essential' or 'indispensable'. Bass continuo means—as it sounds—continuous bass and would have been provided in this case by a cello or viola da gamba and an organ or harpsichord or both. In obbligato playing it is important to know the vocal line (on the piano here) as well as your own, and be aware when you are accompanying and when you take over the solo line. Generally Bach writes *p* for the obbligato instrument when the voice is singing and *f* when it is the oboe solo. (The dynamics in brackets are editorial suggestions.) When accompanying the voice, you must play with the utmost clarity of phrasing and, in order not to drown the vocal line, we would suggest that as a general rule you should play at least one dynamic degree under it whenever you are together. Your understanding of the music will also be greatly helped if you find out the meaning of the words.

Diese Arie aus der Kantate Nr. 89 ist für Sopran, obligate Oboe und Basso continuo. Obligat in diesem Kontext bedeutet "unentbehrlich" oder "unerläßlich". Basso continuo bedeutet – wie es klingt – kontinuierlicher Baß und wäre in diesem Falle von einem Cello oder einer Viola da Gamba und einer Orgel oder einem Cembalo oder beiden gespielt worden. Im obligaten Spiel ist es wichtig, daß du die Vokallinie (hier auf dem Klavier) so gut wie deine eigene kennst, und daß du weißt, wann du begleitest und wann du die Sololinie übernimmst. Im allgemeinen schreibt Bach für das obligate Instrument *p*, wenn die Stimme singt, und *f*, wenn die Oboe solo spielt. (Die Lautstärkeangaben in Klammern sind editorische Vorschläge.) Beim Begleiten der Stimme mußt du äußerst klar phrasieren, und, damit die Vokallinie nicht übertönst, schlagen wir vor, daß du wenigstens einen Lautstärkegrad unter ihr bleibst, wann immer ihr zusammen spielt. Es wird deinem Verständnis für die Musik auch sehr helfen, wenn du dir die Bedeutung der Worte klarmachst.

26. THE KISSCADEE BIRD
Der Kisscadeevogel

ALAN RICHARDSON

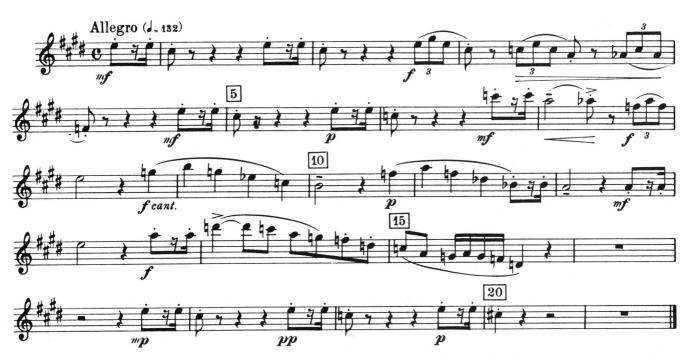

New note: D above the stave (see Appendix).

The Kisscadee bird is native to Trinidad, attractive both in its appearance (bright yellow and black) and in its song, which is imitated in the first three notes of the oboe part. These three notes sound like a question—'Qu'est-ce qu'il dit?'—and from this springs its name. This piece should be played with a very crisp rhythm always showing clearly the difference between

and (otherwise you may get the wrong bird!).

Neue Note: D über dem Notensystem (siehe Anhang).

Der Kisscadeevogel ist in Trinidad heimisch und ist sehr reizvoll im Aussehen (leuchtend gelb und schwarz) und seinem Gesang, der in den ersten drei Noten der Oboenstimme imitiert ist. Diese drei Noten klingen wie eine Frage – 'Qu'est-ce qu'il dit?' – und von daher stammt sein Name. Dieses Stück sollte mit einem sehr klaren Rhythmus gespielt werden, der den Unterschied zwischen und immer deutlich sein läßt (sonst erwischst du vielleicht den falschen Vogel!).

22

27. TRIO
(from *Symphony No. 96 in D major*)

FRANZ JOSEPH HAYDN
(1732–1809)

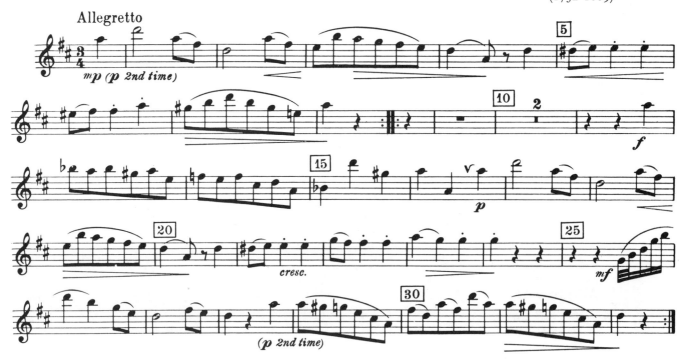

This is the Trio from the Minuet and Trio in what is often called the 'Miracle' Symphony. Like so many of Haydn's trios this needs a graceful dance-like character. The *f*s and *p*s are Haydn's marks; all other marks are editorial.

Practise carefully some legato broken chords up to D in all the keys that D is included. This will help to improve your passage work in bars 7 and 25. Incidentally count the rests carefully in bars 24 and 25; there can be a temptation to come in a little early—resist it!

Dies ist das Trio vom Menuett und Trio der Symphonie, die oft 'Wunder' – Symphonie genannt wird. Wie so viele von Haydns Trios muß auch dieses mit einem graziösen, tanzartigen Charakter gespielt werden. Die *f*s und *p*s sind Haydns Angaben; alle übrigen Angaben sind editorisch.

Übe einige legato Arpeggios bis hinauf zu D sorgfältig in allen Tonarten, die D einschließen. Dies wird dazu beitragen, dein Passagenspiel in den Takten 7 und 25 zu verbessern. Übrigens, zähle die Pausen in den Takten 24 und 25 sorgfältig aus; es könnte die Versuchung bestehen, ein bißchen zu früh einzusetzen – widerstehe ihr!

28. THEME AND TWO VARIATIONS
Thema und zwei Variationen
(from *Divertimento No. 13*)

WOLFGANG AMADEUS MOZART
(1756–1791)

D.C. il Tema, ma Allegretto

This Theme and Variations comes from the sextet for 2 oboes, 2 horns and 2 bassoons, K253. All the sextets are very enjoyable to play but require good breathing capacity and lip control. You can help yourself by taking slight breathing spaces between double bars and between variations. Your pianist can assist you in this by contributing unhurried final bars in each case. The dynamics in brackets are editorial—the other marks are Mozart's.

Dieses Thema und Variationen stammt aus dem Sextett für 2 Oboen, 2 Hörner und 2 Fagotte, K253. Alle Sextette machen viel Freude zu spielen, erfordern jedoch gute Atemleistung und Lippenkontrolle. Du kannst dir dies selbst erleichtern, indem du nach Doppelstrichen und zwischen Variationen kleine Atempausen machst. Dein Pianist kann dich dabei unterstützen, indem er die Endtakte jedesmal in gemächlichem Tempo spielt. Die Lautstärkeangaben in Klammern sind editorisch, die übrigen Angaben stammen von Mozart.

Appendix

The fingering system most suited to contemporary needs (i.e. for music written at the present time) is an open top key on the left hand which necessitates half-holing for middle C♯, D and E♭ and D, E♭, E and F above the stave. This system allows the maximum chord possibilities and alternative fingerings. If this system is used, the fingering for C♯ above the stave should be as in (1).

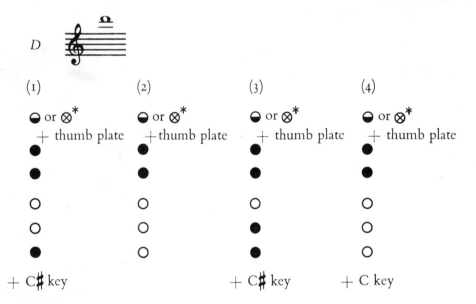

The pitch and also the ease of obtaining the note will vary from instrument to instrument. On most oboes (1) and (3) produce the best tone quality with considerably more 'ring' to the sound.

The pitch and also the ease of obtaining the note will vary from instrument to instrument. On most oboes (2) produces the best tone quality with considerably more 'ring' to the sound.

* The sign ⊗ means that you should take your finger off but that the top key should be adjusted to allow about ½mm of free play. If you have no means of adjusting the key (either by a screw or by fixing cork under the lever behind the key), you must half-hole as in fingering (1), but without pressing too hard with your top finger.

N.B. On most oboes the pitch of these fingerings will vary a little.

19. FRIENDSHIP
Freundschaft
(from *Studies in General Bass*)

GEORG PHILIPP TELEMANN
(1681-1767)

20. AIR
Melodie

HENRY PURCELL
(1659-1695)

21. HORNPIPE
(from *A Midsummer Night's Dream*)

HENRY PURCELL
(1659–1695)

22. ADVENTURE IN STACCATO

Abenteuer in Stakkato

ALAN RICHARDSON

23. DOWN THE VALLEY

Das Tal hinunter

ALAN RICHARDSON

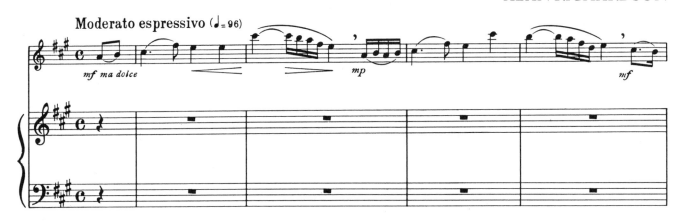

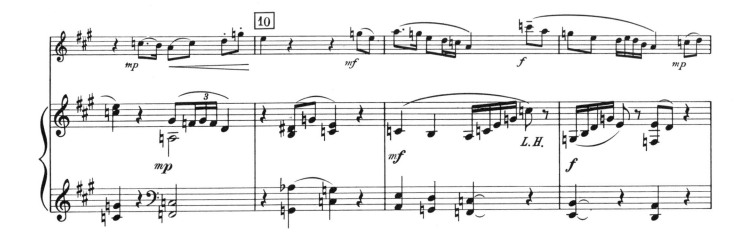

24. L'AMOUR DE MOI

FRENCH TRADITIONAL
arr. A.R.

25. GERECHTER GOTT, ACH, RECHNEST DU?

(from *Cantata No. 89*)

JOHANN SEBASTIAN BACH
(1685–1750)

*Play thus:

26. THE KISSCADEE BIRD

Der Kisscadeevogel

ALAN RICHARDSON

27. TRIO
(from *Symphony No. 96 in D major*)

FRANZ JOSEPH HAYDN
(1732–1809)

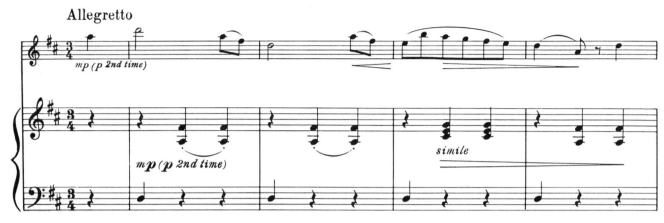

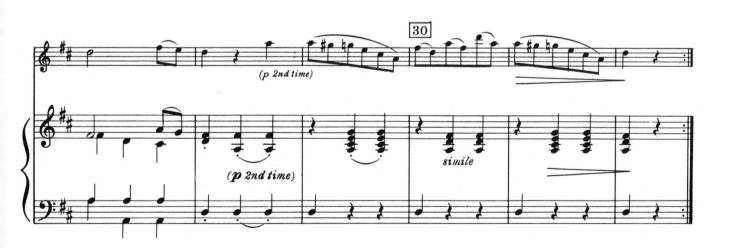

28. THEME AND TWO VARIATIONS

Thema und zwei Variationen

(from *Divertimento No. 13*)

WOLFGANG AMADEUS MOZART
(1756-1791)

Var. **1**

38

Var. 2

D.C. il Tema, ma Allegretto

New note: A above the stave.

The long phrase-marks here show the overall lengths of the phrases; make the joins between the shorter slurs as legato as possible but give clear definition to the notes marked ⌒. Both repeats should be played. To help the rhythm in bars 9-11, think at first in quavers but take care that there are no bulges on the crotchets. When using the 2nd octave key make as little movement of the hand as possible—the slightest rocking action is all that is required. The trill in the last bar can be played faster than suggested provided the quaver D is full length (the piano trill in bar 8 should conform to the oboe trill).

New note: low C.

Let this flow along. The phrasing is important: ⌒ means give a melodic stress to the first note and shorten the second without tongueing it. You can use a very soft tongueing action between the slurs especially at bars 3-4 and 9-12. Begin the piece with sufficient tone in *mf* to allow room for a good contrast when you come to the *p* in bar 9. Always remember that dynamics are relative, and therefore in most cases it is the contrast that is important. Use a very round embouchure (lip formation) for the low C.

Try to make the *fps* expressive rather than hard. They should sound rather like deep quick sighs, and should not be so very much stronger than the up-beat to bar 25. The last 4 bars plus up-beat quaver should, of course, start strong and almost angry.

New note: B flat above the stave.

Oboist and pianist should take great care to phrase alike here. Try playing the Da Capo very quietly throughout with a diminuendo over the last 4 bars, remembering that quiet playing requires plenty of firm support from the diaphragm. The trills may be played as shown or faster, provided the quaver after the trill is full length.

Very legato tongueing is needed throughout this lovely piece. Remember that it is a song and needs to be played as you would sing it. The notes may seem simple but to give full beauty and meaning to them requires much thought, very careful listening and considerable breath and lip control. If you find a diminuendo on the low G difficult, try adding your E flat key (and even the F key as well), which will help to keep the pitch up and give you confidence to diminuendo.

Play the grace-note acciaccaturas (bars 6 and 13) rather quickly but very clearly, and finger them out (no trill keys!). The breath marked in bar 8 should be taken very quickly and must not disturb the crescendo. (Listen to the way good singers snatch a breath without breaking a phrase.) Practise the semiquaver passage in bar 14 until you get it very smooth and clean. This piece could be repeated without a rit the first time.

All the pieces so far have been in the most usual time-signatures, with 2, 3, 4 or 6 beats to a bar. However, composers quite often write in 5/8 or 7/8, etc.; none of us has any difficulty in counting up to 5 or 7, so playing this correctly should not present too much of a problem. Just be careful that you *do* think in 5.

This is the theme from *Don Giovanni* that Beethoven used for his *Variations* for two oboes and cor anglais. We hope that one day you will have the chance of playing the whole work in its original form, and also the Trio in C, Op.87. We suggest the grace-note acciaccatura in bar 4 should be played just before the beat. You will probably have to snatch a breath in bar 18, but be careful not to interrupt the flow of the phrase. Start by playing the trills in bars 22 and 24 as suggested. When your fingers become more agile you can add more notes to the trill, using the trill key in bar 24.

9. New note: B above the stave.

   Play this cantabile but be very careful of the phrasing. The staccato quavers should not be too short. If you can hear an untidy sound between B and C sharp in the middle of the instrument, make up some exercises for yourself using these notes legato. This, of course, applies to any other combinations of notes over the break, such as C-D, C-E flat, B-D, etc. To obtain a good round quality of tone on the B above the stave, you must avoid pinching with the embouchure and give plenty of support from the diaphragm.

10. Play the mezzo-staccato notes ⌒ as cantabile as you can without losing the definition. Remember that if you are playing in a resonant hall or room more definition (or separation) is needed than in a small, heavily curtained and carpeted room. Listen for the grace-notes in the piano part leading into the 13th and the last bars.

11. New note: low C sharp.

    You will probably notice that low C sharp has a quality different from its neighbours, especially from C and D. It is not usually one of the oboe's best-sounding notes and needs a lot of 'nursing' to improve its quality. For all low notes it is necessary to use a very round embouchure, but for C sharp it must be a *very* round one!

12. Ornamentation of melodic lines (such as trills, turns, any added decorations or variations) was customary in Handel's day, and if the player did not ornament it would be assumed that the composer had failed to inspire him! We have suggested some possible ornaments and variants in the repeats and recommend that eventually you try to make versions of your own. Remember that whatever you play must fit with the keyboard-part (i.e. the harmony) and that it should be in the style of the piece. It will help if you play the piece several times in its original form before you add much, apart from trills or mordents. When you have become familiar with this procedure, try to make ornamented repeats for the *Ayre* by John Blow (No. 1), and also for the Da Capo of Purcell's *Rondeau* (No. 4) and later for the *Affettuoso* by Telemann (No. 14).

13. New Note: C above the stave.

    Let this piece flow along without being fast. Notice how the music begins on the 2nd beat of the bar thus giving it a slightly unusual rhythmic feeling.

14. *Affettuoso* means affectionately and, although it is not a tempo indication that we use now, it was used often in Telemann's day, particularly by Telemann himself. It is not a fast tempo and an andante quaver beat would be right here.

    A special word to the pianist (and oboist). We have given the figured bass, indicating the harmony, here and in the Allegro following. The custom in Telemann's day would have been for the keyboard player to play from the figured bass only and for him to harmonize (realize) the part as he went along. We have given a suggested realization. Always remember that the bass line is a duet with the solo part and should be dynamically equal to it, but the right hand part must be at least one dynamic degree down from this, except where the solo part is resting.

15. Make the rhythm here very vital and pointed, with the dotted notes almost double dotted. Notice the many changes of mood and make these changes very clear by playing the dolce sections very dolce to contrast with the precise rhythmic figuration.

16. In bars 1, 3 and 7 we find another mezzo-staccato figure ⌒ ; the C should be slightly lifted and separated from the following note which needs gentle tongueing. Remember to use your L.H. E flat key whenever the E flat precedes or is preceded

by D flat. Match the sounds and intonation of the notes throughout so that we hear no unwritten accents or stresses.

17. If you find any of the passage-work difficult, try practising it in different rhythms, while retaining the written phrasing.

Bars 5-8, for example: ♩ ♪ ♩ ♪ ♩. ♪. ♩. ♪ etc. and
♫. ♫. ♫. ♫. etc.

So long as you keep the rhythms very tight and your fingers very relaxed, this should quickly help you to improve your finger technique. All detached quavers and crotchets should be played rather short.

18. This theme requires the utmost singing-tone and legato phrasing; again it gives good practice in using the L.H. D sharp key. Don't forget that you will need plenty of firm support from the diaphragm in your *pp* phrase at the end. If you fail to provide enough support the phrase will sound tentative and frail instead of controlled and quiet.

19. The changes of time, from 2/4 to 3/8 and from 3/4 to 9/8, may present some difficulties at first. To ensure that the quavers are equal in value (♪ = ♪), begin by thinking in quavers throughout until the changes become familiar. Pianists should take special care to count 9 quavers in bar 14.

20. One of our favourite melodies in this book, this *Air* must be played with great control, and above all with the utmost love and affection. The trills in bar 20 and 23 could be played as in the *Rondeau* (No. 5) or you can trill faster and stop on the dot (in this case the 2nd beat). When you play the repeat don't forget to try some ornaments and variants.

21. This *Hornpipe* will make a good pair with the *Air* (No. 20) for concerts, private or public. The trills can be fast and should stop on the dot. In each case make a slight diminuendo from the trill through the following two notes.

22. This is just what the title suggests. The tempo can be increased as you get better at controlling your staccato-playing.

23. New note: C sharp above the stave (see Appendix).
Here you have an opportunity to begin a piece without any accompaniment. Try taking a little rhythmic licence (rubato).

24. A beautiful melody, but not such a comfortable key! Take great care of the intonation and tone-quality throughout. If your low A flat sags when played quietly, try adding your E flat key. This can help, but beware of it making the note too bright in quality.

25. This aria from Cantata No. 89 is for soprano, oboe obbligato and bass continuo. Obbligato means in this context 'essential' or 'indispensable'. Bass continuo means—as it sounds—continuous bass and would have been provided in this case by a cello or viola da gamba and an organ or harpsichord or both. In obbligato playing it is important to know the vocal line (on the piano here) as well as your own, and be aware when you are accompanying and when you take over the solo line. Generally Bach writes *p* for the obbligato instrument when the voice is singing and *f* when it is the oboe solo. (The dynamics in brackets are editorial suggestions.) When accompanying the voice, you must play with the utmost clarity of phrasing and, in order not to drown the vocal line, we would suggest that as a general rule you should play at least one dynamic degree under it whenever you are together. Your understanding of the music will also be greatly helped if you find out the meaning of the words.

26. New note: D above the stave (see Appendix).
The Kisscadee bird is native to Trinidad, attractive both in its appearance (bright yellow and black) and in its song, which is imitated in the first three notes of the oboe part. These three notes sound like a question—'Qu'est-ce qu'il dit?'—and from this springs its name. This piece should be played with a very crisp rhythm always showing clearly the difference between ♫ ♪ and ♪♪♪ (otherwise you may get the wrong bird!).

27. This is the Trio from the Minuet and Trio in what is often called the 'Miracle' Symphony. Like so many of Haydn's trios this needs a graceful dance-like character. The *f*s and *p*s are Haydn's marks; all other marks are editorial.

Practise carefully some legato broken chords up to D in all the keys that D is included. This will help to improve your passage work in bars 7 and 25. Incidentally count the rests carefully in bars 24 and 25; there can be a temptation to come in a little early—resist it!

28. This Theme and Variations comes from the sextet for 2 oboes, 2 horns and 2 bassoons, K253. All the sextets are very enjoyable to play but require good breathing capacity and lip control. You can help yourself by taking slight breathing spaces between double bars and between variations. Your pianist can assist you in this by contributing unhurried final bars in each case. The dynamics in brackets are editorial—the other marks are Mozart's.

Neue Note: A über dem Notensystem.
Die langen Phrasierungsbögen zeigen hier die Gesamtlänge der Phrasen an. Mache die Verbindungsstellen zwischen den kürzeren Bögen so legato wie möglich, spiele jedoch die durch ⌢ ⌣ gekennzeichneten Noten klar und bestimmt. Beide Wiederholungen sollten gespielt werden. Denke, um mit dem Rhythmus in den Takten 9-11 besser zurechtzukommen, zunächst in Achteln, passe jedoch auf, daß die Viertel dann kein Anschwellen im Ton zeigen. Bewege die Hand bei der Verwendung der zweiten Oktavklappe so wenig wie möglich – eine äußerst geringe Schaukelbewegung, das ist alles, was verlangt ist. Der Triller im letzten Takt kann schneller als vorgeschlagen gespielt werden, vorausgesetzt, daß dem Achtel D der volle Wert gegeben wird (der Klaviertriller in Takt 8 sollte dem Oboentriller entsprechen).

Neue Note: tiefes C.
Lasse dieses Stück dahinfließen. Die Phrasierung ist wichtig: ⌢ ⋅ bedeutet: gib der ersten Note einen melodischen Akzent und verkürze die zweite, ohne sie anzustoßen. Zwischen den Bögen, besonders in den Takten 3-4 und 9-12, kannst du einen sehr sanften Zungenanstoß verwenden. Beginne das Stück mit genügender Tonstärke in *mf*, um Spielraum für einen guten Kontrast zu lassen, wenn du zum *p* in Takt 9 kommst. Vergiß nicht, daß Lautstärken relativ sind, und daß daher in den meisten Fällen der Kontrast das wichtige ist. Verwende für das tiefe C einen sehr runden Lippenansatz.

Versuche, die *fps* eher ausdrucksvoll als hart zu spielen. Sie sollten mehr wie tiefe, schnelle Seufzer klingen und nicht sehr viel stärker sein als der Auftakt zu Takt 25. Die letzten 4 Takte zusammen mit dem Achtel des Auftakts sollten natürlich energisch und beinahe zornig beginnen.

Neue Note: B über dem Notensystem.
Oboist und Pianist sollten sich große Mühe geben, hier übereinstimmend zu phrasieren. Versuche, das Da Capo durchweg sehr leise zu spielen, mit einem diminuendo in den letzten 4 Takten, wobei du daran denken mußt, daß leises Spiel viel starke Unterstützung vom Zwerchfell erfordert. Die Triller können wie angegeben oder schneller gespielt werden, vorausgesetzt, daß das Achtel nach dem Triller seinen vollen Wert behält.

Während dieses ganzen Stückes braucht man einen sehr legato Anstoß. Denke daran, daß es ein Lied ist und so gespielt werden muß, wie du es singen würdest. Die Noten mögen einfach erscheinen; es bedarf jedoch guten Überlegens, viel aufmerksamen Zuhörens und beachtlicher Atem – und Lippenkontrolle, um ihnen volle Schönheit und Bedeutung zu geben. Wenn du ein diminuendo auf dem tiefen G schwierig findest, mache den Versuch, deine Es-Klappe (und sogar auch die F-Klappe) mitzuverwenden, die dabei helfen wird, die Tonhöhe oben zu erhalten und dir Selbstvertrauen zum diminuendo geben wird.

Spiele die ornamentalen Acciaccaturen (Takte 6 und 13) ziemlich schnell, aber sehr klar, und greife sie (keine Trillerklappen verwenden!). Das Atemholen, das in Takt 8 angegeben ist, sollte sehr schnell geschehen und darf das crescendo nicht stören. (Höre dir an, wie gute Singer schnell Atem holen, ohne die Phrase zu unterbrechen.) Übe die Sechzehntelpassage in Takt 14, bis du sie sehr flüssig und sauber spielen kannst. Dieses Stück könnte wiederholt werden, wobei man das rit. beim erstenmal wegläßt.

Alle bisherigen Stücke hatten die gebräuchlichsten Taktangaben, mit 2,3,4 oder 6 Zählzeiten pro Takt. Komponisten schreiben jedoch ziemlich oft in 5/8 oder 7/8 usw.; keiner von uns hat irgendwelche Schwierigkeiten bis 5 oder 7 zu zählen, und so sollte es kein zu großes Problem sein, dieses Stück richtig zu spielen. Passe lediglich auf, daß du *tatsächlich* in 5 denkst.

8. Das ist das Thema aus *Don Giovanni*, das Beethoven für seine *Variationen* für zwei Oboen und Englischhorn verwendete. Wir hoffen, daß du eines Tages die Gelegenheit haben wirst, das ganze Werk in seiner Originalfassung zu spielen, und ebenso das Trio in C, op. 87. Wir schlagen vor, daß die ornamentale Acciaccatura in Takt 4 knapp vor der Zählzeit gespielt wird. Du wirst wahrscheinlich in Takt 18 schnell Atem holen müssen; passe jedoch auf, daß du den Fluß der Phrase nicht unterbrichst. Spiele die Triller in den Takten 22 und 24 anfangs wie vorgeschlagen. Wenn deine Finger flinker werden, kannst du mehr Noten in den Triller aufnehmen und in Takt 24 die Trillerklappe verwenden.

9. Neue Note: H über dem Notensystem.
Spiele dieses Stück cantabile, aber achte sehr auf die Phrasierung. Die Stakkatoachtel sollten nicht zu kurz sein. Schreibe dir, wenn du einen unsauberen Klang zwischen H und Cis in der Mitte des Instruments hörst, selbst ein paar Übungen auf, die diese Noten legato verwenden. Dies gilt natürlich auch für alle anderen Notenkombinationen über dem Registerwechsel, wie C-D, C-Es, H-D usw. Um beim H über dem Notensystem eine gute, runde Tonqualität zu erreichen, mußt du viel Unterstützung vom Zwerchfell geben und es vermeiden, mit dem Lippenansatz zu quetschen.

10. Spiele die Mezzostakkato-Noten ⌢ ⋅ ⋅ ⋅ ⋅ so cantabile wie du es vermagst, ohne daß die Noten an Präzision verlieren. Denke daran, daß, wenn du in einem widerhallenden Saal oder Raum spielst, mehr Präzision (oder Trennen der Noten) vonnöten ist, als in einem kleinen Raum mit schweren Vorhängen und dicken Teppichen. Horche auf die Verzierungsnoten in der Klavierstimme, die in den 13. Takt und die letzten Takte leiten.

11. Neue Note: tiefes Cis.
Du wirst wahrscheinlich bemerken. daß das tiefe Cis eine von seinen Nachbarnoten, vor allem C und D, verschiedene Tonqualität hat. Es ist in der Regel nicht eine der bestklingenden Noten auf der Oboe und braucht eine Menge "Pflege" zur Verbesserung seiner Qualität. Bei allen tiefen Noten ist es notwendig, einen sehr runden Ansatz zu verwenden, für das Cis jedoch muß er ein *sehr* runder sein!

12. Verzierungen von melodischen Linien (wie Triller, Doppelschläge, jegliche hinzugefügte Ausschmückungen oder Variationen) waren zu Händels Zeiten üblich, und wenn der Spieler keine Verzierungen spielte, wurde angenommen, daß es dem Komponisten nicht gelungen war, ihn zu inspirieren! Wir haben einige mögliche Verzierungen und Varianten in den Wiederholungen vorgeschlagen und empfehlen, daß du schließlich versuchst, eigene Versionen anzufertigen. Denke daran, daß alles, was du spielst, zur Klavierstimme (d.h. der Harmonie) passen muß, und daß es im Stil des Stückes sein sollte. Es wird von Nutzen sein, wenn du das Stück einige Male in seiner originalen Fassung spielst, bevor du, abgesehen von Trillern, Pralltrillern und Mordents, viel hinzufügst. Wenn du mit dieser Verfahrensweise vertraut bist, könntest du versuchen, verzierte Wiederholungen für das *Ayre* von John Blow (Nr. 1), und ebenfalls für das Da Capo von Purcells *Rondeau* (Nr. 4) und später für das *Affettuoso* von Telemann (Nr. 14) anzufertigen.

13. Neue Note: C über dem Notensystem.
Lasse dieses Stück dahinfließen, ohne zu hasten. Beachte, wie die Musik auf der zweiten Zählzeit des Taktes beginnt und ihm so ein leicht ungewöhnliches rhythmisches Gefühl verleiht.

14. *Affettuoso* bedeutet innig, und obwohl es keine Tempoangabe ist, die wir jetzt gebrauchen würden, wurde es zu Telemanns Zeiten oft als solche verwendet, besonders von Telemann selbst. Es ist kein schnelles Tempo, und ein Andante, gezählt in Achteln, wäre hier richtig.

Ein besonderes Wort an den Pianisten (und Oboisten). Hier und in dem folgenden Allegro haben wir den bezifferten Baß, der die Harmonie bezeichnet, angegeben. Zu Telemanns Zeit wäre es für den Spieler des Tasteninstruments Brauch gewesen, nur vom bezifferten Baß zu spielen und beim Spielen selbst die Stimme zu harmonisieren (auszusetzen). Wir haben eine von uns vorgeschlagene Aussetzung des Basses angegeben. Vergiß nie, daß die Baßlinie ein Duett mit der Solostimme darstellt und ihr von der Lautstärke her entsprechen sollte; die Stimme der rechten Hand muß jedoch wenigstens einen Lautstärkegrad leiser sein, außer wenn die Solostimme eine Pause hat.

15. Gestalte den Rhythmus hier sehr lebendig und pointiert, und spiele die punktierten Noten fast doppelt punktiert. Beachte die vielen Stimmungswechsel und bringe diese Wechsel sehr deutlich heraus, indem du die dolce Abschnitte im Gegensatz zu der präzisen, rhythmischen Figuration sehr dolce spielst.

16. In den Takten 1. 3 und 7 finden wir eine weitere Mezzostakkato-Figur ♪⌒ ; das C sollte leicht angehoben und von der folgenden Note getrennt werden, die einen sanften Zungenanstoß verlangt. Vergiß nicht, die Es-Klappe der linken Hand immer dann zu verwenden, wenn das Es einem Des vorangeht oder nachfolgt. Stimme die Klänge und Intonationen der Noten durchweg aufeinander ab, so daß wir keine nicht angegebenen Akzente oder Betonungen hören.

17. Solltest du einige der Passagen schwierig finden, so mache den Versuch, sie in verschiedenen Rhythmen zu üben, wobei du die angegebene Phrasierung beibehältst. Takte 5-8 z.B.

♪. ♪ ♪. ♪ ♪. ♪ ♪. ♪ usw.Und ♪♪. ♪♪. ♪♪. ♪♪. usw.

Solange du die Rhythmen sehr genau einhältst und die Finger sehr entspannt, sollte dir dies schnell dabei helfen, deine Fingertechnik zu verbessern. Alle nicht gebundenen Achtel und Viertel sollten ziemlich kurz gespielt werden.

18. Für dieses Thema benötigt man einen äußerst singenden Ton und eine gebundene Phrasierung; es stellt wiederum eine gute Übung in der Verwendung der Dis-Klappe der linken Hand dar. Vergiß nicht, daß du in deiner pp Phrase am Ende viel kräftige Unterstützung vom Zwerchfell brauchen wirst. Wenn du nicht genug Unterstützung zur Verfügung stellst, wird die Phrase wie ein Versuch und schwach, anstatt kontrolliert und leise klingen.

19. Die Taktwechsel von 2/4 nach 3/8 und von 3/4 nach 9/8 werden anfangs vielleicht einige Schwierigkeiten bereiten. Um dafür zu sorgen, daß die Achtel gleichwertig sind (♪ = ♪), solltest du zunächst durchweg in Achteln denken, bis die Wechsel vertraut sind. Die Pianisten sollten in Takt 14 besonders darauf achten, daß sie 9 Achtel zählen.

20. Dieses *Air*, eine unserer Lieblingsmelodien in diesem Buch, muß mit großer Kontrolle, und vor allem mit größter Liebe und Zuneigung gespielt werden. Die Triller in den Takten 20 und 23 können so wie im *Rondeau* (Nr. 5) gespielt werden, oder du kannst schneller trillern und auf dem Verlängerungspunkt aufhören (in diesem Fall der 2. Zählzeit). Vergiß nicht, einige Ornamente und Varianten zu probieren, wenn du die Wiederholung spielst.

21. Dieser *Hornpipe* und das *Air* (Nr. 20) werden zusammen ein gutes Paar für Konzerte zu Hause und in der Öffentlichkeit abgeben. Die Triller können schnell sein und sollten auf dem Verlängerungspunkt aufhören. Spiele jedesmal ein leichtes diminuendo vom Triller über die nächsten zwei Noten hinweg.

22. Dies ist genau das, worauf der Titel anspielt. Du kannst das Tempo mit fortschreitender Kontrolle deines Stakkatospiels beschleunigen.

23. Neue Note: Cis über dem Notensystem (siehe Anhang).
Hier hast du eine Gelegenheit, ein Stück ohne Begleitung zu beginnen. Mache den Versuch, dir eine kleine rhythmische Lizenz zu erlauben (rubato).

24. Eine schöne Melodie, aber keine so bequeme Tonart! Gib dir mit der Intonation und der Tonqualität durchweg viel Mühe. Mache, wenn dein tiefes As beim Leisespielen im Ton absinkt, den Versuch, deine Es-Klappe hinzuzunehmen. Das kann Abhilfe schaffen, aber paß auf, daß es die Note nicht zu hell klingen läßt.

25. Diese Arie aus der Kantate Nr. 89 ist für Sopran, obligate Oboe und Basso continuo. Obligat in diesem Kontext bedeutet "unentbehrlich" oder "unerläßlich". Basso continuo bedeutet – wie es klingt – kontinuierlicher Baß und wäre in diesem Falle von einem Cello oder einer Viola da Gamba und einer Orgel oder einem Cembalo oder beiden gespielt worden. Im obligaten Spiel ist es wichtig, daß du die Vokallinie (hier auf dem Klavier) so gut wie deine eigene kennst, und daß du weißt, wann du begleitest und wann du die Sololinie übernimmst. Im allgemeinen schreibt Bach für das obligate Instrument *p*, wenn die Stimme singt, und *f*, wenn die Oboe solo spielt. (Die Lautstärkeangaben in Klammern sind editorische Vorschläge.) Beim Begleiten der Stimme mußt du äußerst klar phrasieren, damit die Vokallinie nicht übertönst, schlagen wir vor, daß du wenigstens einen Lautstärkegrad unter ihr bleibst, wann immer ihr zusammen spielt. Es wird deinem Verständnis für die Musik auch sehr helfen, wenn du dir die Bedeutung der Worte klarmachst.

26. Neue Note: D über dem Notensystem (siehe Anhang).
Der Kisscadeevogel ist in Trinidad heimisch und ist sehr reizvoll im Aussehen (leuchtend gelb und schwarz) und seinem Gesang, der in den ersten drei Noten der Oboenstimme imitiert ist. Diese drei Noten klingen wie eine Frage – 'Qu'est-ce qu'il dit?' – und von daher stammt sein Name. Dieses Stück sollte mit einem sehr klaren Rhythmus gespielt werden, der den Unterschied zwischen ♪ ↰ ♪ und ♪♪♪³ immer deutlich sein läßt (sonst erwischst du vielleicht den falschen Vogel!).

27. Dies ist das Trio vom Menuett und Trio der Symphonie, die oft 'Wunder' – Symphonie genannt wird. Wie so viele von Haydns Trios muß auch dieses mit einem graziösen, tanzartigen Charakter gespielt werden. Die *fs* und *ps* sind Haydns Angaben; alle übrigen Angaben sind editorisch.
Übe einige legato Arpeggios bis hinauf zu D sorgfältig in allen Tonarten, die D einschließen. Dies wird dazu beitragen, dein Passagenspiel in den Takten 7 und 25 zu verbessern. Übrigens, zähle die Pausen in den Takten 24 und 25 sorgfältig aus; es könnte die Versuchung bestehen, ein bißchen zu früh einzusetzen – widerstehe ihr!

28. Dieses Thema und Variationen stammt aus dem Sextett für 2 Oboen, 2 Hörner und 2 Fagotte, K253. Alle Sextette machen viel Freude zu spielen, erfordern jedoch gute Atemleistung und Lippenkontrolle. Du kannst dir dies selbst erleichtern, indem du nach Doppelstrichen und zwischen Variationen kleine Atempausen machst. Dein Pianist kann dich dabei unterstützen, indem er die Endtakte jedesmal in gemächlichem Tempo spielt. Die Lautstärkeangaben in Klammern sind editorisch, die übrigen Angaben stammen von Mozart.

Appendix

SOME SUGGESTED FINGERINGS FOR C SHARP AND D ABOVE THE STAVE

The fingering system most suited to contemporary needs (i.e. for music written at the present time) is an open top key on the left hand which necessitates half-holing for middle C♯, D and E♭ and D, E♭, E and F above the stave. This system allows the maximum chord possibilities and alternative fingerings. If this system is used, the fingering for C♯ above the stave should be as in (1).

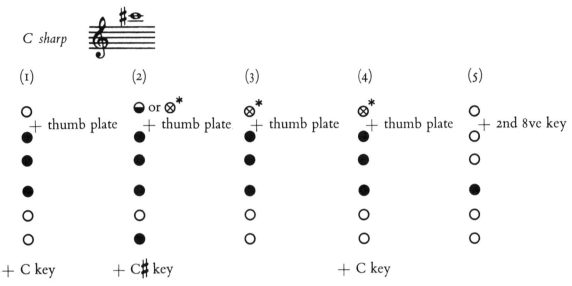

The pitch and also the ease of obtaining the note will vary from instrument to instrument. On most oboes (1) and (3) produce the best tone quality with considerably more 'ring' to the sound.

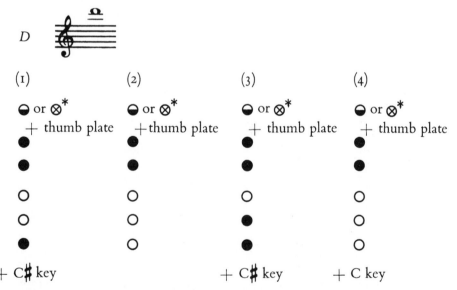

The pitch and also the ease of obtaining the note will vary from instrument to instrument. On most oboes (2) produces the best tone quality with considerably more 'ring' to the sound.

★ The sign ⊗ means that you should take your finger off but that the top key should be adjusted to allow about ½mm of free play. If you have no means of adjusting the key (either by a screw or by fixing cork under the lever behind the key), you must half-hole as in fingering (1), but without pressing too hard with your top finger.

N.B. On most oboes the pitch of these fingerings will vary a little.

Anhang

EINIGE VORSCHLÄGE ZUM GREIFEN VON CIS UND D ÜBER DEM NOTENSYSTEM

Das Griffsystem, das für zeitgenössische Erfordernisse am besten geeignet ist (d.h. für Musik, die jetzt geschrieben wird), ist eine offene oberste Klappe der linken Hand, die ein Schließen des halben Tonloches für Cis′, D′ und Es′ und D′′′, Es′′′, E′′′ und F′′′ erfordert. Dieses System erlaubt die meisten Akkordmöglichkeiten und Alternativgriffe. Wird dieses System verwendet, so sollte die Griffweise für Cis′′′ wie in (1) sein.

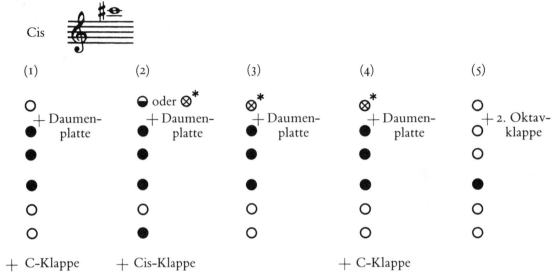

Die Tonhöhe, und auch die Leichtigkeit, mit der die Note erreicht wird, werden von Instrument zu Instrument verschieden sein. Bei den meisten Oboen geben (1) und (3) die beste Tonqualität, mit beträchtlich mehr 'Schall' beim Klang.

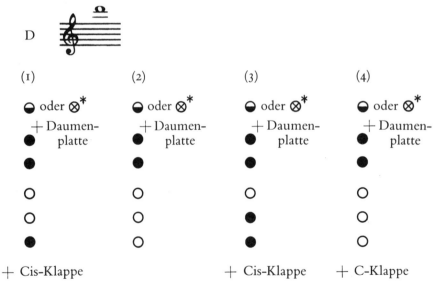

Die Tonhöhe, und auch die Leichtigkeit, mit der die Note erreicht wird, werden von Instrument zu Instrument verschieden sein. Bei den meisten Oboen gibt (2) die beste Tonqualität, mit beträchtlich mehr 'Schall' beim Klang.

★ Das Zeichen ⊗ bedeutet, daß du deinen Finger wegnehmen sollst, wobei jedoch die oberste Klappe so reguliert sein sollte, daß sie etwa ½mm Spielraum hat. Wenn du keine Mittel zur Verfügung hast, die Klappe zu regulieren (entweder mit einer Schraube, oder indem du ein Stück Kork unter dem Hebel hinter der Klappe anbringst), mußt du das Tonloch wie in Griffweise (1) halb greifen, ohne jedoch mit deinem obersten Finger zu hart zu pressen.

N.B. Bei den meisten Oboen werden sich die Tonhöhen je nach Griffweise ein bißchen voneinander unterscheiden.